GETTING TO KNOW OUR PLANET
AMAZON RAIN FOREST

BY VICKY FRANCHINO

Published in the United States of America by Cherry Lake Publishing
Ann Arbor, Michigan
www.cherrylakepublishing.com

Content Adviser: Linda M. Hooper-Bùi, PhD, Associate Professor, Department of
Environmental Science, Louisiana State University Agricultural Center, Baton Rouge, Louisiana
Reading Adviser: Marla Conn, Read With Me Now

Photo Credits: Cover and page 1, © iStockphoto.com/edsongrandisoli; page 5,
© Frontpage/Shutterstock.com; pages 7 and 9, © Dr. Morley Read/Shutterstock.com;
page 11, © soft_light/Shutterstock.com; page 13, © Janossy Gergely/Shutterstock.com;
page 15, © Evikka/Shutterstock.com; page 17, © John L. Absher/Shutterstock.com; page 19,
© FCG/Shutterstock.com; page 21, © John Michaels/Alamy Stock Photo.

LIBRARY OF CONGRESS CATALOGING-IN-PUBLICATION DATA
Franchino, Vicky.
   Amazon Rain Forest / by Vicky Franchino.
      pages cm.—(Community connections) (Getting to know our planet)
   Includes bibliographical references and index.
   ISBN 978-1-63470-513-4 (lib. bdg.)—ISBN 978-1-63470-573-8 (pdf)—
ISBN 978-1-63470-633-9 (pbk.)—ISBN 978-1-63470-693-3 (ebook)
   1. Rain forests—Amazon River Region—Juvenile literature. I. Title.
   QH112.F73 2016
   577.340981'1—dc23   2015027422

Cherry Lake Publishing would like to acknowledge the
work of The Partnership for 21st Century Skills. Please
visit www.p21.org for more information.

Printed in the United States of America
Corporate Graphics
January 2016

AMAZON RAIN FOREST

CONTENTS

A WARM, WET JUNGLE

The Amazon rain forest is one of the most amazing places on Earth. It is a huge jungle filled with insects, plants, and animals. It rains nearly every day in the Amazon. Some parts of the rain forest get more than 100 inches (254 centimeters) of rain each year. Bring a raincoat if you travel there!

The Amazon rain forest is located along the Amazon River in South America.

Are you ready to learn about the Amazon rain forest? Write down what you already know about it. Then write down any questions you have. See if you can find the answers in this book!

Like many rain forests, the Amazon is near the **equator**. This is an imaginary line located around the middle of Earth. It is very warm near the equator. Temperatures in the Amazon are usually about 80 degrees Fahrenheit (27 degrees Celsius) during the day. It stays warm all year long. It is also quite **humid** in the rain forest. The air is heavy and damp.

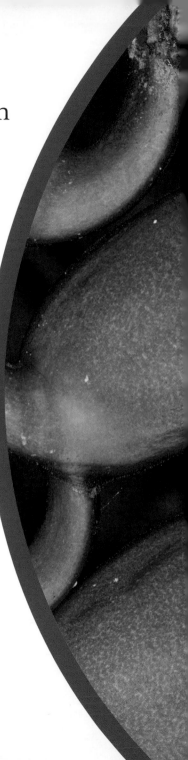

Many plants and animals are suited to the warm, wet environment of the rain forest.

How do the temperature and humidity where you live compare to the rain forest **biome**? What clothes and supplies would you need to bring if you traveled to the Amazon?

FOUR LAYERS

The Amazon rain forest has four layers. The bottom layer is the forest floor. It is dark and moist there. The understory is the layer between the ground and the treetops. Plants in this layer have big leaves. This helps them absorb as much sunlight as possible.

Different plants live at different levels of the rain forest.

Rain, sunlight, and temperature affect the types of plants that can grow in different places. Which plants grow near your home? Do you think they could survive in the rain forest? Could rain forest plants live in your backyard?

The canopy is the leafy roof of the rain forest. It is very thick. This keeps wind, sunlight, and rain from reaching the layers below. Above this is the emergent layer. The rain forest's tallest trees are found here. One type is the ceiba tree. It can be up to 200 feet (61 meters) tall. It grows more than 10 feet (3 m) in a year!

The rain forest canopy is thick, leafy, and green.

Trees in the canopy have smooth leaves with pointy tips. These features help the leaves dry quickly when it rains. Why do you think this might be important in a rain forest?

11

ANIMALS IN THE RAIN FOREST

Thousands of animals live in the Amazon rain forest. The harpy eagle lives in the tallest treetops. It swoops down to catch its **prey**. In the canopy level, you will find toucans, monkeys, and sloths. Some animals spend their entire life in the canopy. They can find food and shelter there. They can also avoid **predators**!

Sloths spend almost all of their time resting in the treetops.

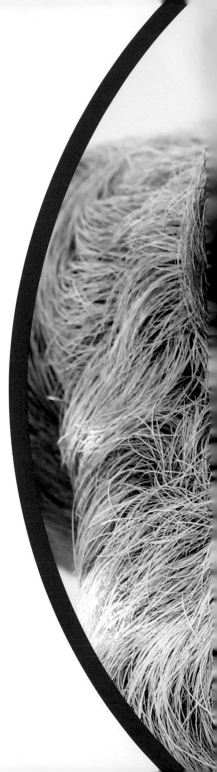

It can be hard for scientists to study animals that live in the canopy. Why do you think this is? What tools could scientists use to learn about life in the Amazon?

13

Many of the animals in the Amazon are dangerous. Jaguars have teeth that are strong enough to bite through a turtle's shell. Boas and anacondas are snakes that squeeze prey to death. There are dangerous creatures in the water, too. Piranhas are fish with razor-sharp teeth. Electric eels can produce electricity five times as strong as a wall socket!

Piranhas may look like regular fish, but they can be very dangerous.

Many animals in the Amazon rain forest are **endangered**. What are people doing that could put these animals in danger? What can people do to protect animals?

15

There are millions of insects in the Amazon rain forest. The titan beetle is one of the largest. It can be as long as an ice-cream sandwich. Its jaws are strong enough to break a pencil. Leaf-cutting ants are also very strong. They can carry 20 times their weight. Other insects use **camouflage**. The owl butterfly tricks predators into believing it is a bird.

The wings of an owl butterfly look a lot like an owl's face.

Search for insects that live near you. Look in trees and under plants. What do these insects have in common with ones that live in the Amazon? How are they different?

17

PEOPLE OF THE AMAZON

Much of the Amazon rain forest is wilderness. There are few roads. Boats are the only way to travel in many areas. However, more than 20 million people live in the Amazon rain forest today. About half of them live in cities. They have modern homes. They use electricity, cars, and computers.

Manaus, Brazil, is one of the biggest cities in the Amazon.

Try drawing a picture of an interesting part of the rain forest. There are lots of ideas to choose from. You could draw animals that live in the Amazon's different layers. You could also draw an insect that uses camouflage, or a rain forest village. Choose whatever interests you most!

Other people live in tiny villages. Some **indigenous** people still live the way their **ancestors** did. They know how to survive in the rain forest. They use local animals and plants for food and medicine.

The Amazon rain forest is a mysterious and beautiful place. Would you like to live there?

An indigenous fisherman casts a net in a river in the Amazon Rain Forest.

THINK!

How would life in a rain forest village be different from life in your town? Where would you sleep? What kind of food would you eat? What would your house look like?

GLOSSARY

ancestors (AN-ses-turz) members of a family who lived long ago

biome (BYE-ohm) a type of area on Earth that is organized by which plants and animals live there

camouflage (KAM-uh-flahzh) a disguise or natural coloring that allows animals, people, or objects to hide by making them look like their surroundings

endangered (en-DAYN-jurd) at risk of dying out completely

equator (i-KWAY-tur) an imaginary line around the middle of Earth that is equal distance from the North and South Poles

humid (HYOO-mid) humid weather is moist and usually very warm

indigenous (in-DIJ-uh-nuhs) native to a country or area

predators (PRED-uh-turz) animals that live by hunting other animals for food

prey (PRAY) an animal hunted by another animal for food

FIND OUT MORE

BOOKS

Heos, Bridget. *Do You Really Want to Visit a Rainforest?* Mankato, MN: Amicus Illustrated, 2015.

Johnson, Robin. *Rain Forests Inside Out.* New York: Crabtree Publishing, 2015.

Watson, Galadriel. *Amazon Rain Forest.* North Mankato, MN: AV2 by Weigl, 2012.

WEB SITES

National Geographic Kids: Amazon Facts!
www.ngkids.co.uk/places/amazon-facts
Check out photos and fun facts about the Amazon.

San Diego Zoo: Tropical Rain Forest
http://animals.sandiegozoo.org/habitats/tropical-rain-forest
Learn more about the animals that live in the tropical rain forest.

INDEX

ABOUT THE AUTHOR

Vicky Franchino has written dozens of books about the natural world and was very excited to learn about the Amazon rain forest. She does not want to see a titan beetle close-up (but her friend Alex, who wants to be an entomologist when he grows up, thinks it would be great fun!). Vicky would like to live someplace that doesn't have winter, but the Amazon rain forest would be very far from Wisconsin where she lives with her family.